Richard Slee

Ceramics in Studio

John Houston

Bellew Publishing CC

First published in Great Britain in 1990
by Bellew Publishing Company Limited
7 Southampton Place, London WC1A 2DR

This book was funded by the Crafts Council

Designed by Ray Carpenter

British Library Cataloguing in Publication Data
Houston, John, *1935-*
    Ceramics in studio: Richard Slee. – (Craft in studio).
    1. English ceramics. Slee, Richard
    I. Title II. Series
    738.092

    ISBN 0 947792 47 3

Title page: drawing, leaf vase 1984-5

This page: drawing, Paisley bowl 1984-5

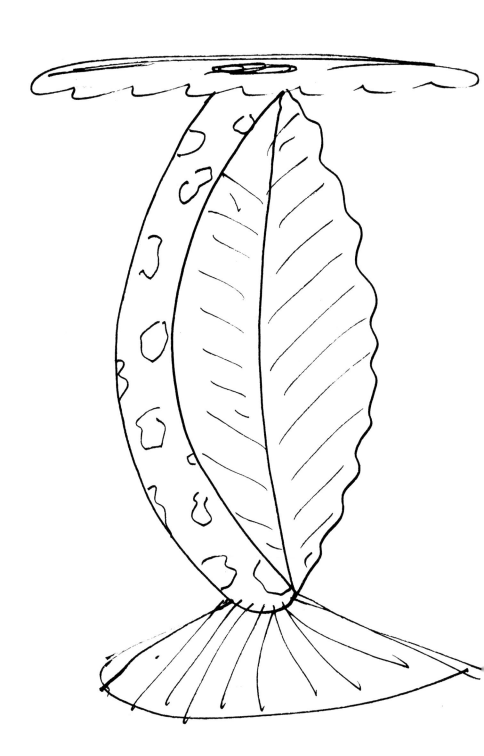

Contents

Drawings for goblets with
handles 1984-5

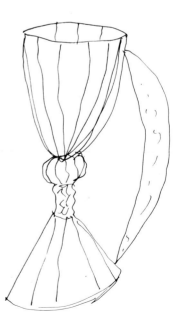

RICHARD SLEE is a craft potter (he is firm about this) and not a ceramist, ceramic sculptor, or any kind of designer ('I don't work to a brief'). Because there is an ounce of orthodoxy in even the most intransigent ex-art student, the formal concerns of the twentieth century aren't evaded, but it's noticeable that he is no Modernist either. Many of the affections and opinions which feed his work are clearly stated in this book, but Slee's Grand Tour doesn't stop at the Bauhaus. His student years perfectly fitted the Pop Art part of the 1960s, when young London swam in a delirium of Style, much of it induced by one of the American Dreams (Home + Her = Heaven) in which Styling seemed to play a decisive role. But Styling – which smoothed and sleeked products heavenwards – was received with ironical enthusiasm by the 1960s Stylists, whose dandyism valued the frivolous above everything. Styling was redefined as entertainment.

Perhaps it's not so very strange to make craft pottery in the second half of the twentieth century? It's low down in the hierarchy of manufactured materials – gold, bronze, silk, crystal . . . lower even than the base metals and the cheating

7

alloys . . . having, in fact, nearly no value at all, other than what the maker adds – rather like the so-called Fine Arts. These 'refined' arts have been dumping their dross for centuries, steadily ditching intrinsically precious materials and their associated skills in order to soar upwards to thoughtful, metaphysical regions. All this prescriptive ballast of trade practices, craft skills and showy substance continued to give great weight to the grander crafts. These came to be called the Lesser Arts in the nineteenth century when all the new classes of society were given, according to status, their own aesthetic aspirations.

The Fine Arts had flown free in the nick of time, for along came the Industrial Revolution with its formidable powers of money and machinery, changing the material order of society, and drowning the old meaningful world of artefacts in a flood of new methods, new categories of production and consumption, and new ways of representing and controlling society. Craft potters, with their tiny margin of profit, were among the first to suffer as lighter, more durable metal goods and changing ways of cooking sliced into their markets. The canniest craftsmen survived by becoming purveyors of entertainment to the new middling classes. Their handmade objects (quickly seen to be a sign for past times) served up the recent (and remoter) past as cute tradition, nostalgic notions, faked evidence of a fast-fading agrarian society portrayed by wassail bowls, posset pots, cheery jugs to puzzle or to celebrate the peasant, tygs and porringers for the new connoisseurs of 'curios'.

The main market for these gnarled and charming images of Never-Never Olde Englande was among the new suburbanites whose glistening villas had been crisply tiled and crockeried by the great industrial potteries. Their tender status confirmed by the cosmopolitan styling of industrial production, they turned to the craft potter for quaint personality, good old stories, sentimental inscriptions, emblematic forms (animal, vegetable and Royal) and ceramic qualities that firmly said 'Earthenware, colourful, historic'. Craft pottery had survived as their story-teller. It continues to offer handmade ceramic qualities, coated with social and historical texture. These objects, like muddy stones, are potentially alive, with an ecology of narrative and audience. That's entertainment.

Richard Slee has a few more options than those earlier craft potters who were squeezed into quirky corners where they could only sell colourful tales to townies.

He teaches in English art schools for three days each term-time week. These schools, first created over 150 years ago to assist the manufacturing industries, are also the main protector of the surviving crafts. Slee is also part of that internationalism which uses craft in much the same way as medieval scholars used Latin: to profitably roam colleges, arts centres and conferences where craft is shown and spoken. So much for narrative and audience (an expert audience of insiders). So much for money. That leaves the pots and the potters free. As Slee says: 'There are *no* set rules . . . just consider formulations like "the independent craftsman". There's no point – unless you *are* independent, in which case the formula is nonsense.'

Teaching the craft of pottery should be the same, he claims: 'I'm very conscious of trying *not* to set rules. I suppose I do demand a level of competence – craftsmanship's different, because it can be interpreted in so many different ways.' It's no joke to suggest that teaching and making are two different kinds of cultivation. The teaching seems very like the old craft potter's extensive vegetable garden: reports suggest that Slee tends to his teaching with a vegetable gardener's fierce devotion to growth and results. The difference is that Slee's artefacts are portrayals of more personal states, of those fiercer and funnier and unfair imaginings that work well above and below the level of competence.

The heart of this book is an edited version of Slee's self-description. The language is candid, cranky, and disarmingly cautionary. I've said elsewhere that his objects carry the full force of his spiky personality: they shrewdly mock, themselves, their craft and frequently their maker. All true. Slee finds it monstrous and funny that ceramic goblets form part of the current craft repertoire – and glues a silver one on to a ceramic cask to mock a time when he was drinking heavily. He loves the worthlessness of ceramic (and is suspicious of all the guru-ology, and sacred technologies, and the Holy Ghost-ism of certain subtle adorings of those – but not these – absolute ceramic qualities) and studs his most ornamental jars with shiny ceramic 'jewels'. A ceramic anvil – symbol of Socialism in decline – marks a period of frustration, but it's downright silly, and funny as well. His ability to be cynical, silly, and shrewd – all at the same time, in both an artefact and a conversation – suggests fast and clever connections. Fancy footwork? I propose, admiringly, the soft-hearted dandy: the aesthete for

9

whom Style is still Entertainment, especially when he cares about the subject.

Even the candour may be part of a selected and well-rehearsed persona, because his self-description (self-deprecating though it is) is the admitted product of a hundred art-school slide presentations 'The Work – The Life'. The inevitable comparison arises: between that Ancient Potterer selling his colourful tales to townies, and Slee, twinkling in the projector's beam and volunteering the secret life of objects – an entertaining *son et lumière* for us arties.

It's the stuff of craft pottery that both should want to entertain. But the senior man was at the end of an old cheerful humanizing craft, and at the end of his wits, too, in looking for new material. He was a generalist: swapping Lord Nelson's head for last year's hero, dressing an obelisk with newer victory swags, pressing type into clay to name a betrothal dish; he sold simple, ornamental certainties. Literacy has weakened our response to those figurative groups. But Slee, deriving much of his pottery language from the gloss and precision of the great industrializing potteries of the eighteenth and nineteenth centuries, has evolved new ornaments which fit his wryly personal histories. Despite their ornamental nature his artefacts are unable to conceal states of heart and states of mind. They are deliberated indiscretions, always working against the grain of his source material, but finding odd compatabilities – between Victorian cover-ups and Disney's biological quirks; between the skeletal and the sentimental; between candour and cliché.

Slee's formal etiquettes corset turbulent contradictions. He suspects that Surrealism has been his best bad example, with its elective affinity for all psychological and aesthetic deliriums. He has a sure hand with the delusive conjunction, the textures that waver between suavity and surgery, the pulsing Victorian gourd betrayed by a crisp webbed foot and a lid like a sexual regatta – all flutter and froth. How this happens, how artefacts can be psyched-up into this animated state, is well described by Edward Allington in the 1985 catalogue of British Ceramics on show at the Museum Het Kruithuis in s'Hertogenbosch:

'It is his enthusiasm for animated graphics, and the works of that nervous surreal genius of the comic strip George Herriman, that allows us to gain some insight into the very contemporary value of Slee's work. When starting a piece

Slee draws the intended form, repeating the image until the rendition becomes almost automatic, like the gradually changing cells that constitute an animated film. Slee uses the technique of this modern medium to convert a pottery tradition, as many potters throw and rethrow the same form to achieve one pot as the finished piece, to achieve the frozen moment. In Herriman's famous Krazy Kat strip the three principal characters, locked in a curious love triangle, act out their rivalries in front of bizarre backgrounds which change erratically from frame to frame (mountains, walls, potted plants and complete landscapes change, appear, or disappear as the plot unfolds), making the characters and their very human condition seem eternal against a speeded-up and ever-changing backdrop of history.'

Allington goes on to suggest that Slee's ceramics, so laboriously made and yet animated and articulated by a single fluid image, can be seen in the same light as Herriman's unstable world. Slee's artefacts are his characters 'disquieting and out of place . . . but belonging to some other very familiar backdrop that has only just changed'.

Finally, Slee's objects convey moods. They do it enjoyably. Their aesthetic presence is a matter of carefully considered relationships: not Modernist statements, but well observed and illustrated equivalents for details of temperament and sensibility. Such observation is disarming, which is just as well, considering some of the moody messages that are conveyed. Intimations of disaster, and Spring; broken hearts and a chipped (but cartwheeling) plate. It was Susan Sontag who said 'Surrealism's great gift to sensibility was to make melancholy cheerful.'

Emblematic, bloody-minded, super-kitsch, this glossy earthenware has got him through a tough decade.

Note on the Captions

All Richard Slee's pots are earthenware. He makes them as
big as the kiln will allow. Up to 1985 that maximum was
related to an 18-inch cube (sometimes fired with the door
open to achieve an extra inch), but from 1985 it has been a
27-inch-high interior.

The scale of his work is important to him. He describes it as
'just about what one would expect it to be (does that make
sense?) but a bit larger'. They do have a surprising presence,
particularly when the object doesn't fit a familiar ceramic
category. An anvil? Slee thinks of the scale as domestic –
that's the environment his objects are intended for,
certainly *not* for museums. However, he admits that the
twentieth-century pots at the Victoria & Albert Museum *are*
much bigger than those made in the previous centuries.
He is doubtful about making smaller things himself 'maybe
because it smacks of the precious', although he concedes
that since Pop Art fashion has favoured a larger scale.
In North America, 'giant' is 'standard'. He believes that the
present scale of his work is OK.

In the end, we chose *not* to caption the objects with their
dimensions.

Richard Slee: Techniques and Bodies

Up to 1977 used Potclay's White St Thomas body (1106),
biscuit-firing to 1160°C. The fired colour was a light buff,
but it had a 'dead ring' and the fired body was too coarse.
In 1977 added two-thirds of Potclay's White Earthenware
(1140) to one-third of White St Thomas; the clay had less
plasticity but it was workable. The fired body colour was
lighter. Biscuit-firing is at 1160°C, followed by glaze
(sprayed) firing at 1040°C. Pieces are often glazed more
than once. Since RCA degree project (1986–8) has developed
his own clay.

The technique is hand-building: coiling, slabbing and
modelling. Textures are press-moulded or modelled. Other
decoration by drawing, coloured clays, slips, under-glaze
colour and crayon, and the occasional use of enamel colours.

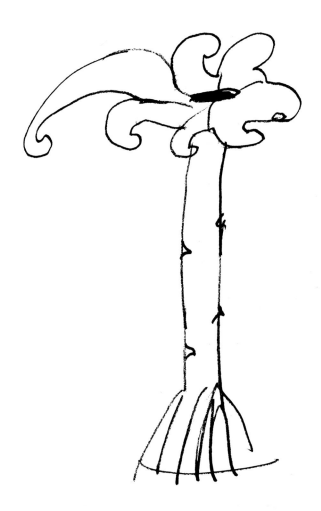

Richard Slee in his own words

This is an edited version of several hours of conversation which circled around 'the prepared lecture' – his words for the bio-pic of slides and recollection that he has developed in his travels as visiting artist, guest lecturer, itinerant teacher. As such, it's a very informal representation: a lively, sketchy performance in which the work and the person provide ambiguous interpretations of each other.

"*By developing certain monstrosities we obtain the purest ornaments*"

Jean Genet

Drawing of cornucopia with legs 1984-5

I LEFT SCHOOL with an 'A' level in Engineering Graphics and got a job as a roadsweeper – a job I'd had before in the summer holidays. I didn't know what I was doing. At the end of August my father had a quiet word with me and said 'Are you going to do that for the rest of your life?' My father was an accountant in local government. He said 'I know people in insurance, or in the local bank' . . . Out of desperation I tried the art college (in Carlisle, where I lived) and got on to the Foundation Course. It was a revelation: for the first time you were treated like an individual. I got on really well and got into the Central School (of Art and Design) in London. That was 1965.

I'd enrolled for the Industrial Design course, which was awful, but switched to Ceramics after a term. It didn't put me off the Central because I knew I wanted to be in London more than anything else. That first dreadful term I just wandered around Soho. It was a good time, generally, with lots of really new work being made, and lots of encouragement. I had a year off before my final year at the Central. When I came back to London it was terrific, I had this much greater clarity, not so much about what I was *going* to do, as about the *way* to work. I realized that they couldn't *physically* stop me doing anything that I wanted, as long as I worked. I didn't worry about what I'd do later, whether I'd be a potter or something else. The activity, the education – they were the important things. There were no set rules that said you had to have a career, or must have your first one-man show by a certain time.

That's one of the things I still think about – even though you become part of the establishment yourself – that there are *no* set rules. I don't think I act on it enough. It's a good response to everything. Just consider a formulation like 'the independent craftsman'. There's no point – unless you *are* independent, in which case the formula is nonsense. It's a worrying thing being *part* of something. I'd come to London as a student, and stayed on to work, to be part of something that's going on. But the danger, as I came to see it, was that it's so easy just to be following on. That's why I moved to Brighton at the end of the 1970s. I wanted to test myself out. Brighton is hardly the Himalayas, but I wanted to see if I could exist independently of fashion. So very easy to pick it up in London. Not so easy in Brighton; and I wanted to find out if I did have something to say for myself.

But! Still in London in 1970–1 I worked for eighteen months as a designer-technician for the Electric Colour Company – a not quite hippy commune. It was begun by Andrew Greaves, a sculptor and photographer from Derby Art School, and some ex-St Martin's School of Art people. They were all four or five years older than me. We did mixed design: shops – the original Mr Freedom in the King's Road – flats, furniture, jewellery and customized cars. It was all very Pop Art imagery, in a workshop off Liverpool Street. All very shambolic, but very enjoyable. Towards the end of that I also did some part-time teaching, in the evening.

Then I worked, as a slave, for a potter in Croydon. The principal event was making a mural of her design for either a Wimpy bar or a Golden Egg restaurant. I recall Roman scenes, gladiators, cut-outs of half-size figures with melted glass islands.

In the summer of 1971 I lived at Dan Arbeid's and used his studio. After leaving Dan's I got a job as a technician with Jerome Abbo at the Central School. After about a term he went to the pottery course at Harrow and I took over as technician and as a tutor. I worked there for eighteen months, making my pots there in my spare time.

1. Three pots with handles
1972 stoneware

2. Wavy pots with lids
1971 stoneware

3. Jig-saw dogs and grass
1972 stoneware

The work was weighty – some of it even looked like old iron weights, and flat-irons and metal tools. When I was a student a constant criticism was that any piece of pottery was far too heavy. So I thought I'd be deliberate about it. I also liked the idea that these were basic shapes: they worked as basic symbols – like A B C or square, circle, triangle. The container idea was still there. Some were like solid bags, others like handbags . . . A premonition of the Iron Lady. The phrase 'I'll hit you over the head with my handbag' kept repeating itself in my mind while I was making these.

Because I wasn't making a tremendous amount – living in bed-sits – I did a lot of drawing: finished-type drawing. But that drawing is now degenerating, gets worse and worse, is now totally a means of putting down ideas about what I make. I don't do any objective drawing. The drawing that I did was more imaginative, mixed with some kind of collage. It's a pity I don't do it any more.

4. Falling slate teapot
1973 drawing

In 1973, after five months being a technician in Yugoslavia, I came back to England and got a job teaching at Hastings School of Art. I taught a mixture of Foundation, and evening-class people . . . I managed to do a little bit of work in a rented studio. I was two years at Hastings, and halfway through I went to America. I was bowled over. I went to California, and to Los Angeles; briefly into Mexico, which depressed me no end; and I spent five days in Las Vegas which blew my mind, as they say. It was like landing on Mars: five days with the camera glued to my eyeball, taking as many pictures as possible.

One of the things was the crazy geometry. I stayed in California with this illustrator friend who had a big collection of popular ceramics of the 1930s and 1940s. One of the things I enjoyed was this fat, clumsy pottery with little logos and identifying transfers applied in unexpected places: a new kind of scale and proportion for me. They had soft, shiny earthenware glazes over soft contours. The glazes were primary and pastel colours, and some of the forms were the streamlined 'Aerodynamic' style which fits my affection for the Disney animation influence.

Another thing I liked was the refrigerator ceramics, water-coolers and so on; I liked them being free of any tradition. They were designed by people who were obviously much more interested in styling than in ceramics or any tradition in ceramics. They used colour in an amazing way: very simple, but it seemed very radical then. Teapots with a different-coloured lid and spout; fiesta-ware cups and saucers all in different colours. I really drooled over those. It was their fatness and heaviness – the weight thing again.

In 1975 I resigned from Hastings after two years. I'd done part-time the first year, full-time the second. I was getting very miserable because I wasn't doing any of my own work, and the teaching was awful: three-quarters of it was evening classes. Although it did teach me to work fast – either demonstrating or making their work for them out of boredom. But I decided to move back to London. I managed to rent a house from Paul Phelp who was a potter at that time. He made coloured agate earthenware. He had stopped working and was moving to Wales. I moved in with my then girlfriend and spent two years there, looking after the house, just paying the rates. And so I had this wonderful studio and could work for an exhibition.

I came across this gallery which was in Kensington Church Street; Smith & Others. I stood outside it for about an hour, plucked up enough courage to go in, and asked for an exhibition; he gave me one! It was run by Peter Smith, who sold a mixture of ceramics and crafts and odd things. I very much liked the gallery because it was almost like a shop: small, intimate, darkly painted and plain. I only found out much later that it was backed by Christopher Strangeways – as a silent partner. Half of it had

5. Richard Slee's first solo exhibition, 1977. Smith & Others gallery, Kensington Church Street, London

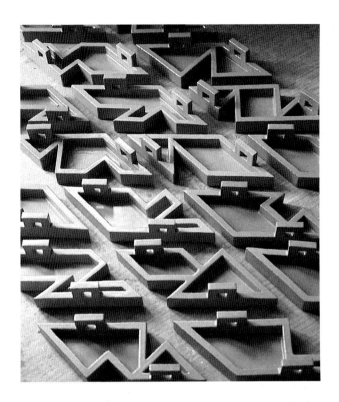

6. Twenty-one trays
1977 earthenware

previously been the Leach pottery's showroom, and Carol McNicoll had her studio at the rear of the shop. I wanted a lot of work in the show, to make the gallery look like a shop, so we displayed things in that stacked kind of way – on shelves and in cupboards.

This was one of the first pieces I made for the show: twenty-one trays, a composite piece. Again its heaviness was important, and so was the idea of secret use. It had a function, but you didn't know what. That came out of Mexican codexes: those wonderful pages that you don't know the meaning of. The permutation came from a Chinese tanagram. The objects were mostly composites: Azteckie things like wheelbarrows, and tools (making pots that looked as though they could perform some service) and Las Vegas geometry, and an animation thing from Disney.

7. Vase with prop
1977 earthenware

The reception was middling. It didn't sell very well, but I got a good response: people were very enthusiastic about it. It was well received by friends and contemporaries, but it wasn't reviewed, which hurt, except for a random comment in *Crafts*: 'Punk pottery . . . dubious aesthetic worth.' But this is where the working career began. I liked the animation and some of the puns: a zig-zag piece in a dish was called 'Flash-in-the-Pan'. You could say it's 'Disney meets Montezuma'. I was making things that were fairly simple. The technique was that I had a dozen or so press-moulds which were simple things, like rings and a few basic shapes. For example, I'd bend a sheet of clay round a rolling-pin to make a tube, have a coiled element as well, and use the press-moulded ring as a collar.

8. Three-part jug
1977 earthenware

9. Multi-colour teapot
1980 earthenware

24

Right. After that show, Paul Phelp sold the studio. It was in Wandsworth. I moved to Hackney and rented a room from friends who'd just bought a house. I had a kiln in an incredibly damp basement and did very little work. Then in 1979 we moved to Brighton, bought a house that was a wreck and spent a year reclaiming bits of it, being a builder for about two years in all. There was no demand for my work. Also there was nowhere for it to go. Smith & Others had closed down, the British Crafts Centre was very conservative, and Strangeways had become giftware. In 1980 I was invited to make a couple of teapots for a group show at the Cleveland Crafts Centre, but that was all. It was not until 1981 that I showed again at Knokke Heist (in Belgium, in the major exhibition of British Ceramics and Textiles) and that led to a show in Holland which was seen by Tatjana Marsden (then manager of the Crafts Shop at the Victoria & Albert Museum). My work took off.

In the three years since the show at Smith & Others I'd thought a lot about the nature of that work, and come to various conclusions. All that early work was earthenware, but I felt that the glazes weren't earthenware, they were masquerading as stoneware, and I felt that the shapes were very stoneware as well. And I didn't any more like things sitting directly on the ground, which is a stoneware convention. I wanted to lift them up. And I thought the matt glazes were too tasteful, owing too much to stoneware again. So I changed the glazes. Another thing was that, since I'd been working with these press-moulds, it had been too easy for me to make work. I'd been collaging: making the bits and sticking them together. I was just accepting what came out of the mould instead of making decisions about scale and so on. It was becoming too clichéd. So I threw away the moulds and I made this teapot – the first time that I'd used actual texture – modelled texture. The colours were lighter, brighter, shinier. And I made this K teapot – which is a homage to Krazy Kat, another early influence.

At the time they seemed to me to be two different things. One was a constructivist teapot, the other was a Pop Art teapot. The two things weren't quite fighting each other but I really didn't know which way to

10. Krazy Kat teapot
1980 earthenware

go. It still felt a bit of a cop-out, because there were still some press-moulded elements, like this ring and other older ways still coming through. But the colour and the shine were just right.

I made this piece and I was very excited. I'd never used texture at all. I was frightened of it somehow, I always wanted things smooth. At last I'd solved this problem. So I started to make these pieces, making texture

with my fingers and by running a tool over the surface. And I began to use glazes more creatively. The earlier work might have had two, even three glazes on one piece, but now I used as many glazes as a piece would take. I refired again and again until I got exactly what I wanted. It was a terrifically creative period.

When I made that first textured pot it reminded me of Victorian ceramics. I started to look at them, reread Pevsner's *Pioneers of Modern Design*. Now when I was a child I had two spinster aunties, one a real aunty. They lived in a terrace house that was full of pottery. One had travelled the world as a nurse and had a tortoise shell from Togo and so on. Terrific. I was fascinated by all their knick-knacks. My grandmother had a similar house-full. But I'd gone to art school and had been imbued with Modernism, so that one felt almost guilty looking at this stuff.

When I reread Pevsner I realized how vitriolic he was about decadence and so on. I started re-examining this decadence in Victorian pottery and discovered people such as Christopher Dresser and Sir Edmund Elton, and got very influenced by the variety and creativity of their shapes and the luxurious glazes. But I was veering between that and the stuff drawn from Krazy Kat territory and popular imagery in general. One thing that I discovered was that my way of building things from separate pieces matched Victorian thinking about pots – everything had its proper zone: foot, neck, body and so on. That was a pleasing similarity.

Another influence in the early 1980s was this Punk thing. I remember working in the studio in the summer and listening to the Brixton Riots on the radio, and thinking that this decadence was very apt for the times. Margaret Thatcher's speech about a return to Victorian values fitted very nicely! This started me off making things in a way that was part experiment and part creative splurge. Jars with lids, such as this painter's jar – the opening is an eye and there's a kind of palette of colour, the colours distinct but also merging. And the jars were lifted by little feet or a foot, so there was very little of the surface that was unglazed. Playing around a lot with texture, with slip under the glaze, with different decorative techniques using slip and latex and crayon. This was a jar I

11. Jar with lid
1981 earthenware

12. Vase
1982 earthenware

29

made as a sample piece. It has four different decorations on its sides: an article of cultural doodles! Then I was putting things on cabriole legs. And here's a smoker's jar. And a more voluminous shape. A lot with both glaze and pressed texture.

The thing is, about those finger-textured pieces, it only works with very soft clay. It's also a bit like the sort of real risk-taking throwing that I enjoy in some Italian peasant pots and in English medieval wares – the volume is light and breathing and just about to collapse. In fact, the way I discovered it in the beginning was that I only had some sticky clay and I wanted to do some work. I started coiling it and it was sticking to my

13. Smoker's jar
1982 earthenware

14. Painter's jar
1981 earthenware

15. Jar with lid
1985 earthenware

hands and I thought it was quite interesting working with this very soft clay. So I worked in front of an electric fire, very quickly, up to a certain point – then dried it off, and continued working. I liked the constraint, that this was the only way that you could work the clay. In fact, now that's the way I always work – I force-dry everything, because I work better if things are all made in a day. If I carry them over I usually lose something.

I don't work in series. I choose pottery-type subjects – dishes, jars, bowls, plates – but I'll make a jar and then I'll make a plate, then something else, then something else . . . I have a personal dislike of exhibitions which are just the same idea in lots of variations. I want to avoid that. Also, I get a break between subjects, which I find is more creative. I have time to digest what I've done and make the next decision. It fits with my affection for collections: things accumulated in real time – like the Willett Collection in the Brighton Art Gallery. Most of my exhibitions have been collections.

The Victorian influence has helped me to look at textile patterns – the Paisley patterns in particular leading on to plates of various types. I quite enjoy making plates, because there are so few hand-built ones around today. I like latching on to subjects where the field's free – there are less contemporary precedents and the barriers are easier to break down. So, I started on plates in various guises – plates and bowls; using pools of glaze. Some of these things would be fired half a dozen times, some even twelve times. I went into Selfridges and there was an exhibition of Chinese reproduction plates. All of them on these little stands. So I came home and made one with a built-in stand. It prompted me to make this plate, the cart-wheeling plate, the happy plate. The raggedy edge is simply because it's been cart-wheeling a long time and gets a bit chipped. I enjoy the whole thing of chipped plates in junk markets – the quality of the chipped edge – and so I built it in.

1981–84 was a good, creative period when I was very happy working. This was in Brighton, in my old house: pre-separation from my wife, so it was pre-1984. I did quite a lot of good work during the separation. It took my mind off the hell that was going on elsewhere.

16. Jar with open-work lid
1981 earthenware

17. Standing plate
1981 earthenware

18. Happy plate
1982 earthenware
Crafts Council Collection,
London

34

19. Bowl
1982 earthenware
Crafts Council Collection,
London

20. Spiral dish
1982 earthenware
Victoria & Albert Museum,
London

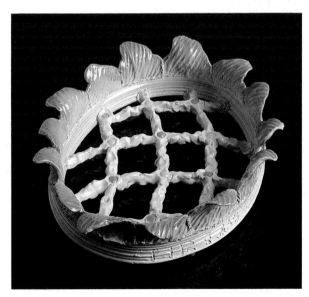

21. Lattice dish
1984 earthenware
Buckinghamshire County
Museum

The Victoriana thing also brought up the cornucopia. I thought 'what a terrific thing' and nobody had made one at that time. It was the decadence-theme continued: Bacchanalian objects! I made them in various disguises – a fossilized cornucopia, one in broderie anglaise, and a 1950s poodle-for-Doris-Day cornucopia.

22. Cornucopia
1984 earthenware

Drawings for winged
cornucopia 1984

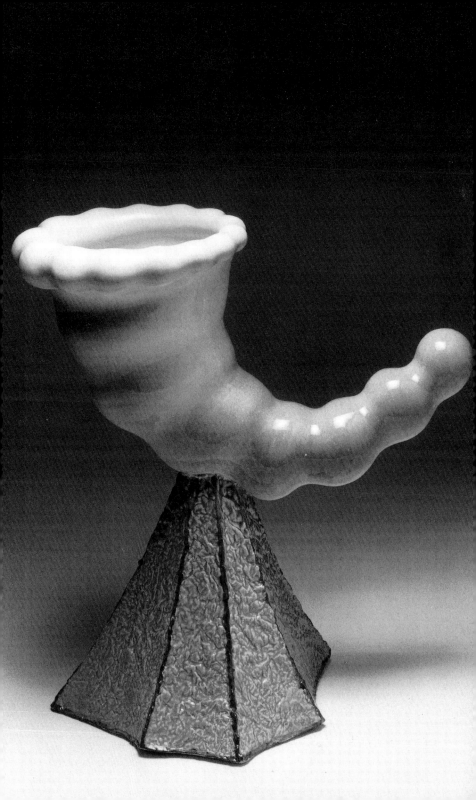

23. Cornucopia
1984 earthenware

24. Cornucopia
1984 earthenware

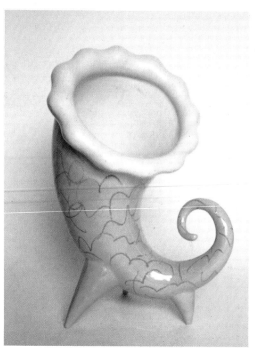

25. Cornucopia
1984 earthenware

26. 'Visage' cornucopia
1986 earthenware

27. The last cornucopia
1984 earthenware

28. Jar with lid
1986 earthenware

I was saying about the drawing. At that time I was often repeating drawings – over and over and over again – to get exactly the drawing that I was pleased with, and then I'd try and build that into the piece. That goes back to my enjoyment of Las Vegas where you get handwriting twenty foot high but there's obviously no giant drawing it out. For all its flowing quality it's quite carefully, laboriously made. That's a misleading, contradictory quality that I like.

Right. 1984. The show at the British Crafts Centre (from 1987 known as Contemporary Applied Arts). I had been showing a lot in group exhibitions, and I'd had little shows at the V&A Crafts Shop, but this was the first major show since Smith & Others in 1977. For the Smith & Others show I had a very clear feeling about the ambience and everything else I wanted, but I didn't know in this case. So I gave myself a theme: I wanted to show my versatility, to have as full a range as possible. I love these jars and have made quite a number of the voluminous ones – sometimes a bit soggy, sometimes puffed-up.

There was a flower, and a dish, and because it was Olympic year, a torch (no one wanted it), and another jar and a pipe. I made one real cornucopia for the show. I was fed-up with making them – the danger bells were starting to ring again – so I called it 'The Last Cornucopia'. I've stripped it of all decoration and put it in jeopardy on this tall stand.

29. Pair of ornaments
1984 earthenware

30. Reclining heart with handle
1985 earthenware

31. Tilted heart dish
1986 earthenware

42

It was also the first time I'd made a piece without an orifice, no reference to pottery form. I talked about it at the time, I wanted such pieces to be seen as part of an ornamental tradition. I began to make pairs of things on the same basis, sometimes not-quite pairs that were mirror-images of each other.

In 1984-6, I worked with simple themes, simple symbolism to do with what concerned me, with things that were happening outside. It's sentimentality, the hearts were obvious at the time of the divorce. Hence these reclining hearts, and a cracked heart dish – a bleeding heart!

I also did a thing on goblets. I find the naffest kind of object you can make in ceramics is a goblet. I can't imagine anybody wanting to drink out of a ceramic goblet. The other reason is that personally I was drinking a lot at this time. So I stuck a goblet on a barrel so you couldn't get it off.

There was also this connection with computer technology. I used to have one – a Sinclair. I remember spending all evening drawing a cube and then revolving it and thinking I could just draw it in any position in two seconds, so why waste time? I was very cynical about it. One of the great things about these early computer graphics was when I went to this demonstration and they drew a goblet. They always drew a goblet! So there it was revolving on the screen, but the computer couldn't fill in the bottom of the bowl. So I made such a goblet – it's hollow all the way through! It also referred to the drinking thing I had then. And I made it all crinkly, so it looked really ancient.

This plate is another symbol of frustration, in a way: the open scissors fitted like a cancellation on the plate. A plate is such a passive object, that to put such a threatening symbol on it was quite a nice combination.

Another theme was crowns: this is a crown and orb partly because I felt that ceramics is such a worthless substance, and I thought of that American phrase about a wooden nickle. It was also at the time of the Royal Wedding and Royal Overkill. So this was my contribution.

This is the anvil, which is partly about frustration. It seemed to me the most frustrating ceramic object you could make: you can't hit it. It was the time that Socialism was beginning to wane, so it's a mourning for that.

32. Pair of hearts
1986 earthenware

33. Scissor plate
1985 earthenware

45

34. Anvil
1987 earthenware

35. Crown and orb
1986 earthenware

In the summer of 1986 I went to America, to this disused brick factory in Maine, the Watershed Centre for Ceramic Arts. It was a factory that had been mothballed for a couple of years. The owner opened it up to be a centre for ceramics, and that's how it's working now. I was one of six or seven people that summer (I went over with Angus Suttie). It was half work, half holiday. I wasn't working for anything – just working. In clay and straw: I hardly fired anything, just one firing. It was play. This is me flying to America.

I had this idea of making large things, an exercise to make things that weren't pots. It was in rural Maine, very, very beautiful; there was a farmer outside making hay, and I decided to use clay and hay together. I couldn't work in my normal way, so it forced me to make altogether different things. There was a six-foot-long needle in a haystack.

After Maine I came back to England, got secondment from Harrow

36. Flying to America
1986 clay and straw

37. Scissors on stand
1986 clay and straw

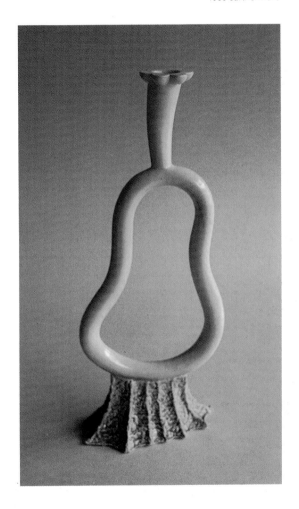

38. Crown and anvil
1988 earthenware

(from teaching on the pottery course at Harrow College of Higher Education) and did an MA by project at the Royal College of Art in London: one year full-time, a second year part-time. The project was to develop a clay body: there were certain technical drawbacks to the one I'd been using. But also I thought about decoration. I'd never really decorated things because I had always found difficulties about drawing on to ceramics. I didn't call it decorating – I called it drawing – partly because so much decorating then was merely facile, a lot of scribbling and splashing. And I was concerned about meaning in decoration.

So I got the clay body I wanted and then decided to play around with various decorative ideas. I decided to make a series of plates, because they were the quickest and easiest things to make. I'd been pleased about the body, because I'm no chemist and I thought I might not have been capable of doing it. But I was disappointed about the plates – I don't think the decorative thing did go very well, although some pieces were OK. But I'll probably go back to it at some point.

The imagery was still partly about the demise of Socialism – hence an anvil, a builder's trowel and a crescent of bricks: a reference to being walled in. The techniques were different sorts of printing: mono-prints, lino-prints, rubber stamps, lots of playing around with those methods. Other imagery came from fruit-machines, and that was partly about the Royal College itself – the yuppie-dom of the place – and about the City – money before everything else. One I liked was a kidney-shaped plate with pattern of kidney-beans: it was very much that fruit-machine imagery: 'You're not worth a bean!' The V&A bought it.

I was still making work here while I was doing the Royal College project. Because my time was divided between two places, there wasn't an enormous amount of new ideas, but a lot of the existing ideas were resolved – got a lot stronger. I began to play around with things *without* bases, the fruitlike forms, such as the pumpkins. And I was simplifying colour a lot, down to about two glazes on a piece. But it was this idea of floor-sculpture that kept going, with thanks and credit to Jacqui Poncelet and Richard Deacon.

40. Flower vase
1987 earthenware

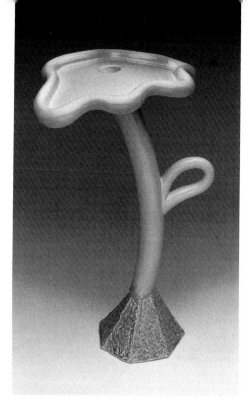

41. Flower vase
1987 earthenware

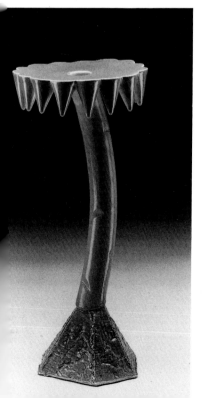

42. Kidney dish
1986 earthenware
*Victoria & Albert Museum,
London*

53

43. Vanishing heart
1988 earthenware

44. Pumpkin
1987 earthenware
*Crafts Council Collection,
London*

45. Leaf
1989 earthenware

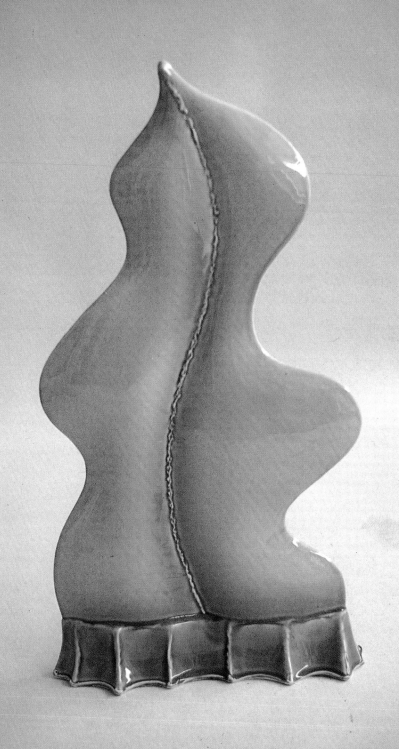

So this is now the beginning of 1989. I'd left the Royal College, I was using the new clay body, which is a lot purer and I can do a lot more with it. I'd also purified the glazes to get sharper, cleaner colours. And I'd looked back at the last four years of work, which had been, for me, a time of pessimism about the world. I was too cynical. After this stocktaking I wanted to make something more optimistic. So I started on this theme of things sprouting, putting out leaves: everything is beginning to sprout; this is Spring!

The kind of thing I'd been looking at was Dutch Delft-ware and Bristol tin-glaze – tiles, all of it so optimistic, and all these lovely drawings of boats and objects are alive because they're contemporary subjects. I did one that was virtually a copy, but then I got my own versions.

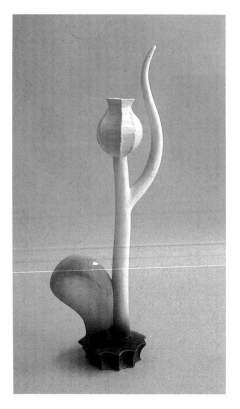

46. Flower
1989 earthenware

47. Spinning plate
1989 earthenware

48. Three flasks
1989 earthenware

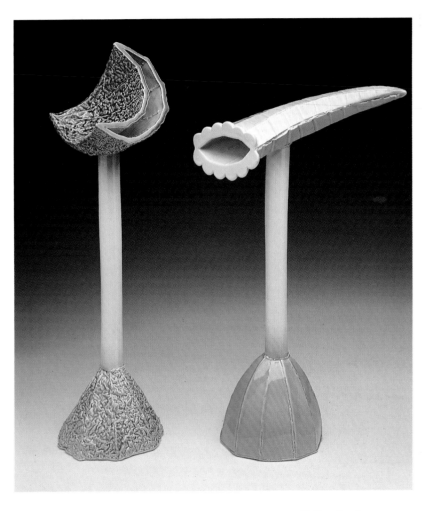

49. Comet and moon
1989 earthenware

So what about influence? I'm more tolerant than I used to be. When people said, 'Who influences you?' I'd answer, 'One person' – and leave it at that! But now it's a matter of whatever you admire may have some effect. But the person who really influenced me was Kenneth Price, and that's because of two shows of his I saw at the Kasmin Gallery (in London's New Bond Street) in the 1960s when I was a student at the Central. I was bowled over by them. The first one was of these moundlike pieces which were sprayed in car enamel. That was so radical to me, coming from this purist ceramic background. It was really 'fuck you!' to the ceramic world. The second exhibition was of the snail cups, only six or eight pieces, but so exotic even in this small gallery. They were behind glass and presented so well, there was something so incredibly special about them. The scale was right, everything was right. I follow everything he does. He makes mistakes sometimes – everybody does, but I think he's the most innovative, the most eloquent ceramicist around. I think now that he was probably the person who convinced me that there was mileage in making ceramics.

Why do I do it? Because I can't find anything else to do. Because I still discover more and more about the inherent qualities of the material. It's been worked on for four thousand years, so it's not very likely that I'm discovering anything new, but as you go on and on you're getting deeper into the material, deeper into the maturity of ideas. And when you're young you can change from day to day: tomorrow I could make furniture, or be a politician, or a mercenary. But now it's not going to be that easy. A year ago I went to my doctor. I was incredibly nervous. I am quite nervous anyway, and I build up a lot of nervous energy. My heart was going too hard all the time. He said, 'What's the matter?' I said, 'It's my teaching job, I'm just totally frustrated all the time, I want out.' And he said, 'Well, what else are you going to do at your age?' It was the best advice I could have had.

Drawings for Paisley pattern bowls 1984

Richard Slee

1946 Born Carlisle, Cumbria
Training
1964–5 Carlisle College of Art and Design
1965–70 Central School of Art and Design,
Dip. AD, first-class honours
Ceramics
1986–8 Royal College of Art, MA Design
RCA. Design by project
1970–1 Designer/technician at Electric
Colour Company, London
1971–3 Ceramic technician, Central
School of Art, London
1973 Ceramic design consultant,
Mural Project, Yugoslavia
1986 Summer guest artist, Watershed
Center for Ceramic Arts, Maine,
USA
Teaching
1973–5 Hastings College of Further
Education, full-time
1975 to Central School of Art and Design
present Harrow School of Art

Exhibitions

1977 **Richard Slee,** solo exhibition,
Smith & Others Gallery, London
British Teapots, Camden Arts
Centre, London
1981 **British 20th Century Studio
Ceramics,** Christopher Wood
Gallery, London
British Ceramics and Textiles,
Crafts Advisory Committee (now
Crafts Council)/British Council,
Knokke Heist, Belgium
Teapots Old and New, Dan Klein,
London
1981–2 **Central Ceramics,** Eton Drawing
School and Central School of Art
and Design, London
1982 **Exhibition 1,** opening show
shared with Ruth Franklin,
Carol McNicoll, Henry Pim,
Angus Suttie, Aspects Gallery,
London

Nonconformists?, show shared
with Vilma Henkelman, Carol
McNicoll, Betty Woodman, Galerie
Het Kapelhuis, Amersfoort,
Netherlands
**Richard Slee, Nicholas Homoky,
Carol McNicoll, Jacqui Poncelet,**
Ceramic Work Centre, Heusden,
Netherlands
1983 **Richard Slee,** solo exhibition,
Crafts Council Shop, Victoria &
Albert Museum, London
Fifty-Five Pots, The Orchard
Gallery, Londonderry, Northern
Ireland
1984 **Richard Slee, Katherine Virgils,**
British Crafts Centre, London
British Ceramics, British Council,
Czechoslovakia
**Three Generations of British
Ceramics,** Maya Behn Gallery,
Zurich, Switzerland
English Ceramics, Charlotte
Hennig Gallery, Worms, West
Germany
1985 **Richard Slee, Alison Britton,
Carol McNicoll, Jacqui Poncelet,**
Galerie Het Kapelhuis,
Amersfoort, Netherlands
British Ceramics, Museum Het
Kruithuis, s'Hertogenbosch,
Netherlands
Fast Forward, ICA London;
Kettle's Yard, Cambridge
Going for Baroque, Midland
Group, Nottingham
Group Show, Blond Fine Art, London
1986 **British Ceramics,** Dorothy Wiess
Gallery, San Francisco, USA
Britain in Vienna, COI, London/
Kunstlerhaus, Vienna, Austria
English Ceramics 1980–5,
Kunstformen Jetz, Salzburg,
Austria
Richard Slee, solo exhibition,
Crafts Council Shop, Victoria &
Albert Museum, London
Made in Britain, Kunsthandwerk,
Berlin, and tour of West Germany

Group Show, Blond Fine Art, London
Staff Show, Central School of Art
and Design, London 1973
New British Design, Spitalfields
Heritage Museum, London 1981
1987 **English Ceramics in Bassano,**
Bassano Del Grappa, Italy
Our Domestic Landscape,
Corner House Gallery, Manchester
and UK tour
**A New Spirit: Contemporary
British Ceramics,** San Francisco
International Airport Arts
Commission, USA
Richard Slee, solo exhibition, 1982
Hodaland Kunstnersentrum,
Bergen, and Gallery F.15 Oslo,
Norway 1983
1988 **East-West Contemporary
Ceramics,** British Council, Seoul,
Korea and Hong Kong
**Sotheby's Decorative Arts
Award Exhibition,** London
Contemporary British Crafts,
British Council/Crafts Council,
National Museums of Modern Art,
Kyoto and Tokyo, Japan
London/Amsterdam, New Art 1984
**Objects from Britain and
Holland,** Crafts Council, London,
Gallery Ra, Gallery de Witte Voet,
Amsterdam, Netherlands
Celebrity Crafts, Usher Gallery,
Lincoln and UK tour
1989 **Richard Slee, Martin Smith,
Richard Meitner, Eko Yoshiya,**
Galerie Het Kapelhuis,
Amersfoort, Netherlands
Richard Slee – Recent Works,
the City Art Gallery, Leicester
British Studio Ceramics,
Buckinghamshire County Museum 1985
1990 **Richard Slee,** solo exhibition,
National Museum, Stockholm, Sweden
Three Ways of Seeing,
Fred Baier, furniture; Caroline
Broadhead, jewellery; Richard
Slee, pottery; Crafts Council,
London and tour

Publications

Slee Notes, Janet Street Porter,
Design No 293 May
British Ceramics, Victor Margrie,
Ceramic Review January/
February
British 20th Century Ceramics,
catalogue, Christopher Wood
Gallery, London
British Ceramics and Textiles,
catalogue, British Council/Crafts
Advisory Committee (now Crafts
Council), Knokke Heist, Belgium
Review of Exhibition 1 at
Aspects, Beatrice Phillpotts,
Arts Review, April
Richard Slee, Richard Slee,
Ceramic Review, January/
February
Sèvres with Krazy Kat, Alison
Britton, *Crafts* No 61 May/April
**Fifty Five Pots and Three
Opinions,** catalogue,
Peter Dormer, Martina Margetts,
Peter Fuller, the Orchard Gallery,
Londonderry, Northern Ireland
Routes of Exchange, Peter
Dormer, *Crafts* No 68 May/June
**The Art of the Double Glazing
Craftsperson,** Peter Dormer,
Art Monthly No 87 April
Richard Slee, Katherine Virgils,
Richard Deacon, Contemporary
Applied Arts, London
**Richard Slee, Katherine Virgils,
Jan Cumming,** *Arts Review* Vol 36
No 10
British Ceramics, catalogue,
Ministry of Culture, Bratislava,
Czechoslovakia
**Getting Away from Chat-Show
Sculpture,** William Feaver,
Observer 21st April
British Ceramics, catalogue,
Museum Het Kruithuis,
s'Hertogenbosch, Netherlands
Fast Forward, catalogue,
Peter Dormer, ICA, London

Going for Baroque, catalogue,
Midland Group, Nottingham

1986 **The New Ceramics,** Peter Dormer,
Thames & Hudson, London
New British Design,
John Thackara and Stuart Jane,
Thames & Hudson, London
Britain in Vienna, catalogue, COI,
London/Kunstlerhaus, Vienna
Made in Britain, catalogue,
Kunsthandwerk, Berlin

1987 **Desired Designs,** *Brutus,* Japan,
May
Our Domestic Landscape,
catalogue, Corner House Gallery,
Manchester
English Ceramics in Bassano,
catalogue, Bassano Del Grappa,
Italy

1988 **Contemporary British Crafts,**
catalogue, Museums of Modern Art
Tokyo and Kyoto
**London/Amsterdam, New Art
Objects from Britain and
Holland,** catalogue, Crafts
Council, Galerie Ra, Galerie de
Witte Voet, Netherlands

1989 **Richard Slee – Recent Works,**
catalogue, Sean Hetterley, the City
Art Gallery, Leicester
British Studio Ceramics, Paul
Rice and Christopher Gowing,
Barrie & Jenkins, London
**Richard Slee, Martin Smith,
Richard Meitner, Eko Yoshiya,**
Galerie Het Kapelhuis,
Amersfoort, Netherlands

Collections

1977 James Mayor gallery, London, *jug*
Knokke Heist Municipality,
Belgium, *lidded jar*
1981 Victoria & Albert Museum,
London, *painter's jar*
1982 Crafts Council, London, *bowl and
cartwheel plate*

Cleveland Crafts Centre,
Middlesbrough, *vase*
1984 Victoria & Albert Museum,
London, *spiral dish*
Prudential Insurance, UK Offices,
cornucopia and yellow pipe
1985 Museum Het Kruithuis,
s'Hertogenbosch, Netherlands,
moon bowl
1986 National Museum, Stockholm,
Sweden, *vase*
1987 Los Angeles County Museum,
USA, *orb*
Bradford City Museum, *lidded jar*
Norwich City Art Gallery, Norfolk
Paisley Museum, Renfrewshire
Stedelijk Museum, Amsterdam,
Netherlands, *tulip*
1988 Buckinghamshire County
Museum, *lattice dish*
1989 Museum of Modern Art, Kyoto,
Japan
Victoria & Albert Museum,
London, *bean plate*

*The works illustrated are from
private collections and the following:*

Max Clendinning
Crafts Council
The Peters Foundations
Jeffrey Pine
Richard Slee
Nelson Woo

Photographic credits

*(references are to caption
numbers)*
David Cripps 8, 12, 14, 21, 34, 43
Richard Davies 26
Andrew Greaves half-title page
Tim Hill 44
Zul Mukhida 11, 13, 16, 17, 22,
25, 29, 31, 33, 41, 42, 47, 48, 49
Unknown photographers 2, 9, 38
All other photographs by
Richard Slee